Cahokia Mounds

digging
for the past

BRIAN FAGAN
General Editor

Cahokia Mounds

Timothy Pauketat
and Nancy Stone Bernard

OXFORD

UNIVERSITY PRESS

For Ernestine and Mary Anne—N. B.
For Regena, Janet, and Alyssa—T. P.

OXFORD
UNIVERSITY PRESS

Oxford   New York
Auckland   Bangkok   Buenos Aires   Cape Town   Chennai
Dar es Salaam   Delhi   Hong Kong   Istanbul   Karachi   Kolkata
Kuala Lumpur   Madrid   Melbourne   Mexico City   Mumbai   Nairobi
São Paulo   Shanghai   Taipei   Tokyo   Toronto

Library of Congress Cataloging-in-Publication Data

Pauketat, Timothy R.
  Cahokia mounds / Timothy R. Pauketat and Nancy Stone Bernard.
    p. cm. -- (Digging for the past)
Summary: Describes what is known of the ancient city of Cahokia, a site
in present-day Illinois which was inhabited by Native Americans from
about 700 A.D. to 1400 A.D., the Mississippian culture of which it was a
part, and the archaeological investigations undertaken there.
Includes bibliographical references and index.
  ISBN 0-19-515810-5 (alk. paper)
  1. Cahokia Mounds State Historic Park (Ill.)--Juvenile literature. 2.
Mississippian culture--Illinois--American Bottom--Juvenile literature.
3. Excavations (Archaeology)--Illinois--American Bottom--Juvenile
literature. 4. Earthworks (Archaeology)--Illinois--American
Bottom--Juvenile literature. 5. Cahokia Mounds State Historic Park
(Ill.)--Antiquities--Juvenile literature. 6. American Bottom
(Ill.)--Antiquities--Juvenile literature. [1. Cahokia Mounds State
Historic Park (Ill.)--Antiquities. 2. Mississippian culture. 3.
Excavations (Archaeology)] I. Bernard, Nancy S. (Nancy Stone) II.
Title. III. Series.
  E99.M6815 P38 2003
  977.3'89--dc22

                                        2003017806

9 8 7 6 5 4 3 2 1

Printed in Hong Kong on acid-free paper

Design: Kingsley Parker
Layout: Lenny Levitsky
Picture research: Gabriel
    Caplan

Cover: In 1921, archaeologist Warren Moorehead (left) examined Cahokia's mounds. His findings prompted him to begin a fundraising drive to preserve the site by turning it into a state park.

Frontispiece: Archaeologists excavate the remains of ordinary houses at Cahokia Mounds in 1985.

Picture Credits: Courtesy of Nancy Stone Bernard 41 (bottom); Cahokia Mounds State Historic Site: cover (background), frontispiece, 1, 8, 13, 22, 25, 27, 31, 32, 39, 40; Cahokia Mounds State Historic Site/Bill Iseminger: 16, 17, 18, 21; Thomas Gilcrease Institute of American History & Art: 11 (right); Illinois State Museum: 19, 20, 23, 24, 28, 30, 34, 37; Illinois Transportation Archaeological Research Program/Tom Emerson: cover (inset), 3; University of Illinos Urbana-Champaign: 36; Laserwords Graphics: 6, 10; Louisiana State Division of Archaeology, Poverty Point Earthworks (John Gibson): 9;; Ohio Historical Society: 11 (left); Courtesy of Timothy Pauketat: 11 (center), 26, 29, 35, 38, 41 (top); St. Louis Art Museum, Eliza McMillian Fund: 14

Contents

Where and When   6

Introduction   8

CHAPTER 1
Those Who Came Before   9

CHAPTER 2
Explorers and Early Archaeologists   14

CHAPTER 3
Racing the Bulldozers   19

CHAPTER 4
Evidence Accumulates   27

CHAPTER 5
The Great Ceremonial Center Disintegrates   37

Interview with Timothy Pauketat   41

Glossary   44

Further Reading   45

Cahokia Mounds and Related Sites
in the American Midwest   46

Index   47

Where and When

Mounds in the Midwest

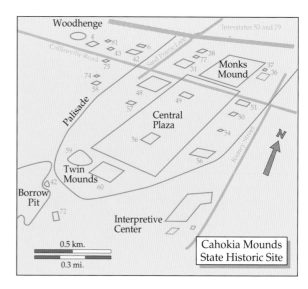

Cahokia Mounds State Historic Site

Archaeological History

1811 ▶
Henry Brackenridge discovers Cahokia site and corresponds with Thomas Jefferson about it

◀ **1860s–1900**
After the Civil War, amateurs and experts map Indian mounds across the United States

1900–1941 ▶
Warren Moorehead excavates at Cahokia in 1920s; Harriet Smith proposes master plan of the site, but her 1941 Cahokia excavations are cut short when United States enter World War II

◀ **1945–1959**
Preston Holder and others excavate Cahokia Mounds, including the first salvage archaeology conducted at Cahokia

1960s ▶
Salvage archaeology is conducted ahead of new interstate highways; woodhenge is discovered

◀ **1970s**
Melvin Fowler discovers Mound 72 burials and Cahokia's great palisade wall; excavation begins as highway construction takes place around the site

1980s ▶
Thomas Emerson and others discover stone figurines depicting Cahokians at farming villages and farmsteads

◀ **1990s**
Timothy Pauketat and others discover more farming villages in the hills around the Mississippi River Bottoms

2000s ▶
Excavations continue

Ancient History

pre–900 CE ◄ Woodland people occupy the Midwestern United States, cultivating food sources, living in small villages or seasonal camps, and building mounds

900–1050 CE ◄ Around the future site of Cahokia, permanent villages begin, population grows based on corn agriculture

1050–1100 CE ◄ Cahokia is founded in a burst of energy around 1050 CE, swells in population up to ten times its former size

1100–1200 CE ◄ Golden age of Cahokia occurs, most mounds are under construction; Ramey Incised pots are made; stone figurines are carved

1200–1275 CE ◄ Palisade walls go up in Cahokia, and some Cahokians leave the area; Cahokia experiences brief stability followed by collapse

1275–1350 CE ◄ Cahokian society collapses, population decreases in large-scale and migration to other areas occurs

1350–1600s CE ◄ A few wandering Indians from the north move through the mostly vacant Mississippi River Bottoms

Introduction

Between 1000 and 1350 CE, long before Europeans landed in the Americas, as many as 16,000 Native Americans lived at Cahokia, with thousands more living in outlying villages. Ruled by powerful chiefs, this great cultural center was a major force along the Mississippi River at this time. The Cahokians built what is now called Monks Mound. At 100 feet high, with a base the size of three football fields, Monks Mound is the highest Indian earthen mound in North America and one of the largest pyramids in the world.

How was Cahokia discovered? How did archaeologists learn who built the mounds and how the Cahokians lived 1,000 years ago? Why did their city collapse? Since the 19th century, archaeologists and curious amateurs have investigated this immense site, and in doing so, they have shown that Cahokia is a true American treasure.

Only eight miles east of St. Louis, Missouri, Monks Mound, built by the Cahokians, is the center of a six-square-mile ancient site of a great North American city that flourished about 1,000 years ago.

1

Those Who Came Before

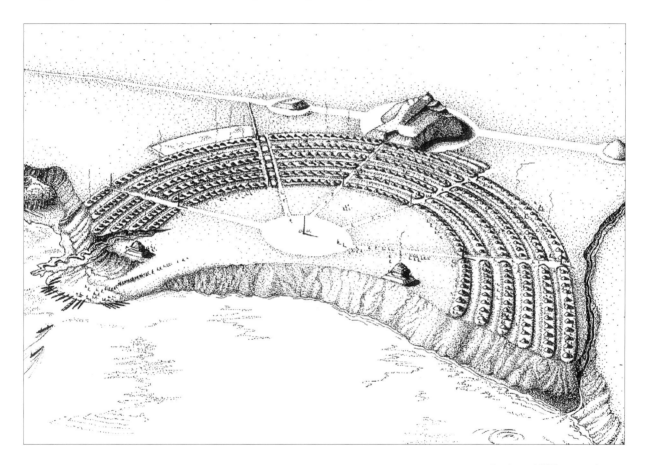

At least 12,000 to 15,000 years ago, small groups of wandering hunters and food collectors known as Paleo-Indians traveled from Asia along the continuous coastline of the Pacific Ocean to the tip of South America, possibly in skin-covered boats. Others walked across the Bering Land Bridge from Asia and proceeded along plains and valleys into North America.

In about 1500 BCE, prehistoric Indians constructed these ridges, measuring one quarter of a mile across, at Poverty Point, Louisiana. These people fished, hunted, and gathered, as well as traded for exotic items from afar.

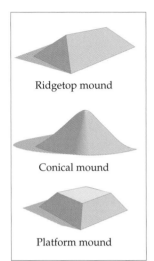

Ridgetop mound

Conical mound

Platform mound

These types of Indian mounds are found at Cahokia and other mound sites.

About 8,000 years ago, during what archaeologists call the Archaic period, Native Americans were hunting, fishing, and collecting the natural bounty of the land. New discoveries show that as early as 6,000 years ago, Archaic hunters and gatherers built mounds in what is now Louisiana. The oldest mounds in the Americas are located at Louisiana's Watson Brake site, ranging from 3 to 25 feet in height. Later, about 3,500 years ago, Archaic people at Poverty Point, Louisiana, constructed enormous semicircular ridges.

By 1000 BCE, cultures that archaeologists call Woodland Indians developed throughout eastern North America. Like the late Archaic people, Woodland Indians cultivated grass seed, squash, and sunflowers native to the Mississippi Valley. More and more, they became an agricultural society, growing, cooking, and storing plant foods using a new technology—ceramic pots.

Mounds for various purposes continued to be constructed in Louisiana and all along the Gulf Coast. Burial mounds were built in the Midwest about 2,000 years ago. The largest of these were in West Virginia, Ohio, and Kentucky. Each mound contained the graves of important family members, buried with large numbers of artifacts.

By 200 CE (1,800 years ago) Woodland Indians built hundreds of burial mounds as well as huge geometric-shaped earthworks that enclosed many acres. In Newark, Ohio, east of Columbus, they carefully designed square, circular, and octagonal earthen enclosures using their own standard unit of measure. Earthen walls ten feet high blocked people on the outside from seeing the activities that went on inside, which probably included sacred ceremonies overseen by shamans (religious leaders). Outside, people built

permanent homes and farmed. Burial goods show that these people, called the Hopewell, made finely decorated pottery and established a long-distance trading network to bring grizzly bear teeth and volcanic glass (obsidian) from what is today Yellowstone National Park, 1,000 miles away. The burial goods also included pendants, ear ornaments, and ritual weapons, hammered into shape from copper nuggets from the Upper Great Lakes, as well as hands, animals, and bird claws, cut into silhouettes from mica, a shiny, flat, mirror-like mineral from the mountains of Virginia and North Carolina. In Iowa, northern Illinois, and Wisconsin, Woodland people built earthworks constructed in the shapes of bears, birds, and geometric figures, called effigy mounds.

By 600 CE, Woodland Indians were using the bow and arrow, and as this new technology swept the continent, societies began to

An eagle talon (left), a mother and her child (center), and a beaver-shaped pipe (right) are examples of thousands of mica, stone, and ceramic artifacts found in mounds at Cahokia and across the Midwest. These items were buried with chiefs and important family members at death.

change. A couple of centuries later, Indians began growing maize, or Indian corn, as a major part of their diet. With it, the populations grew larger. This resulted in a decline on people's health and increased violence between the people of distant villages.

Beginning just before 900 CE, agriculture became the basis for the growth of Woodland villages south along the Mississippi River, including a village where Cahokia Mounds is located. These Indians planted maize, squash, pumpkins, sunflowers, and grass seeds that grew profusely in the hot humid summers on the fertile Mississippi River Bottoms. These crops could be stored easily and could feed a large population. The people supplemented their diet by collecting wild plants and hunting.

Because the Midwestern Indians did not have writing, archaeologists have had to piece together clues to explain what happened next. From excavations, we know that the population of the Woodland villages grew to several hundred people in the Mississippi River Bottoms by 1000 CE. Cahokia was the largest of these settlements with perhaps as many as 1,000 residents.

Sometime prior to 1050 CE, the Cahokians rebuilt their village, perhaps within a few years, into a grand capital with earthen pyramids, spacious plazas, and new houses, all in a flurry of human activity and monument building that North America had not seen before. Soon, this former village had as many as 10,000 to 16,000 residents, and thousands more lived in the surrounding region. It was not until the early 1800s, when Philadelphia's population surpassed 20,000, that there was as large a city as Cahokia north of Mexico.

Today, "Mississippian" is the name that experts call the various sites of Indian people who built the earthen pyramids at Cahokia

and elsewhere after 1050 CE. These sites look like ancient Mexican cities, but from what we now know about the Archaic and Woodland peoples, we can say that mound building was an independently formed tradition in North America, and Cahokia played an important part in the invention of this aspect of Mississippian culture.

An artist re-creates what Cahokia looked like in 1150 CE. Monks Mound (center) dominates the plaza and other mounds.

2

Explorers and Early Archaeologists

As this 19th-century paint-ing of an early archaeologi-cal excavation shows, skele-tons in the mound's lower part were buried earlier than the ones near the top. The skeletons at the top were buried long after the mound was abandoned.

Experts do not know what the residents of Cahokia called themselves. European explorers named the site Cahokia after a small tribe of Indians who lived near the mysteri-ous mounds until the early 1700s. The historical connections between present-day tribes and the Cahokians are difficult to trace. Their descendants are probably scattered among the tribes of the Mississippi River and the Great Plains.

Most explorers bypassed the Cahokia Mounds, or else they thought they were just natural hills covered with trees and grass. Even the careful observers Meriwether Lewis and William Clark, who recorded and charted the territories in the West during their 1803–1806 expedition, did not note Cahokia's mounds when they passed nearby them.

Henry Brackenridge, a friend of President Thomas Jefferson, wrote the first detailed description of Cahokia in 1811. While visiting St. Louis, then called Mound City because of its Indian mounds, he heard that Catholic monks had established a monastery across the Mississippi River near some Indian mounds. As a curious scholar, he wanted to see for himself.

He took a ferry across the Mississippi River to Illinois Town, now called East St. Louis, and walked along Cahokia Creek through wet, swampy lowland. As he emerged from it, he saw a group of about 45 mounds on the plain in front of him. These were the first mounds of the sprawling Cahokia complex, now known as the East St. Louis Site. Brackenridge walked on, following an ancient riverbank studded with pyramid-shaped mounds. After several miles, he came to an even larger group of 120 mounds. In the middle of these stood a 100-foot-high earthen pyramid whose base was at least as big as that of the Great Pyramid in Egypt.

Brackenridge wrote to Jefferson, "What a stupendous pile of earth . . . [I was] struck with a degree of astonishment not unlike that which is experienced in contemplating the Egyptian pyramids. To heap up such a mass must have required years and the labors of thousands." Walking around, he surmised that "a very populous town had once existed here . . . and it could not have been the work of thinly scattered tribes." Despite his discovery, Cahokia was neglected from the time of Brackenridge onward.

In the 1880s, John J. R. Patrick, a dentist from nearby Belleville, Illinois, who was interested in archaeology, hired surveyors to make an accurate map of the land between Cahokia and East St. Louis—now U.S. Route 40, the same trail where Brackenridge walked. Patrick's map showed most of the mounds of Cahokia, as well as the remaining mounds left in East St. Louis and in the city of St. Louis. But by this time, urban developers, railroad planners, and businessmen were already at work leveling many of the mounds.

Most people were not interested in the mounds. In the late-19th century, most Indian tribes, except for a few impoverished groups, had been moved to reservations, and the public could not imagine that Indians could have built impressive mounments. In 1894, government archaeologist Cyrus Thomas conducted a series

By the 1860s, the railroad passed very near Monks Mound. It was just one of the industrial and commercial projects that destroyed many of the mounds in the area.

of digs across the eastern United States that proved Native Americans had built the mounds. But even then the destruction of the mounds did not slow down.

In 1911, a physician named John Francis Snyder formed the Cahokia Mounds Association, an organization that lobbied the Illinois legislature to preserve the Cahokia site. Unusual for his time, Snyder had a lifelong interest in the area's archaeological remains, probably because he had been born in a farmhouse built on the side of a mound just south of Cahokia. Unfortunately, his group could not arouse sufficient public interest or convince the state legislature or the U.S. Congress to make Cahokia a national park. The association's attempt was defeated by an obscure Chicago politician who declared, "My district needs parks for live people, and the guys in that mound are all dead ones."

Auger Tests
Harding Mound 8-4-27

In the 1920s, archaeologist Warren King Moorehead conducted boring and other tests to assess the site. This crew is using an auger, a tool resembling a corkscrew, to drill holes in the ground. Moorehead used the tests to convince the Illinois state legislature that Cahokia's mounds were man-made. His detailed publications are still used today.

Help Save The Cahokia Mounds

Andover, Mass., August 1921

The First National Bank of East St. Louis, Illinois, has kindly agreed to receive checks for the Cahokia Fund.

Men of Illinois should be especially interested in explorations of these mounds, located as they are in your own state. It is proposed to send one of the largest exhibits of specimens to your State Museum at Springfield, and another collection to the Field Museum at Chicago. Without cooperation of Illinois citizens we shall not be able to carry on our researches to the extent desired.

W. K. MOOREHEAD.

Since the enclosed circular has been sent out, a large number of persons and institutions have expressed entire sympathy with the movement to save the Cahokia mounds. Some museums have stated that they could include certain sums in their budgets for 1922. However, few museums can spare any considerable amount of cash during the last half of 1921. Since a number of individuals and museums feel able to contribute from $10 to $50, it is thought best to issue a general appeal and secure a hundred or more small contributions. These added to the Andover grant of $650 should give sufficient to conduct explorations September 1 to November 20. My Department has already spent $418 in a trip to Cahokia, circulars, pictures, and propaganda. This is in addition to the $650 credit

Archaeologist Warren King Moorehead wrote and distributed this pamphlet to urge the Illinois legislature to make Cahokia Mounds a state park.

Finally, after a decade of seeing their efforts thwarted, Snyder and his organization arranged for the distinguished teacher and nationally recognized archaeologist Warren King Moorehead to visit Cahokia. In 1921 Moorehead looked over the site, already threatened by railroads and factories, and he promptly declared that this was the biggest group of Indian mounds he had ever seen.

He printed a pamphlet entitled "Help Save The Cahokia Mounds" and began a fund-raising drive that eventually convinced the Illinois legislature to help. In 1925, the state of Illinois paid $52,110 for 144 acres—a small piece of this enormous site—and Cahokia Mounds State Park was established.

Patrick, Snyder, Moorehead, and others interested in the past saved Cahokia because they knew it was a special place. It would take another generation to excavate the site and learn the details about the largest Indian site north of the Rio Grande River.

3

Racing the Bulldozers

Once the top surface of the excavation site is removed, the crew, on hands and knees, carefully exposes artifacts and features such as house floors and storage pits while a supervisor (right corner) maps what they find.

After Cahokia became established as a state park, amateur archaeologists and interested local residents alerted park archaeologists whenever they heard about commercial threats to the area. In 1940, just outside the park boundary, southeast of Monks Mound, the builder Harry Murdock was about to destroy one of the innermost mounds of Cahokia to make way for

This re-creation at Cahokia Mounds Interpretive Center shows the interior of a Mississippian house, which has a central hearth.

dozens of ranch houses. When he began to level the land, Murdock found human bones. Harriet Smith, a young staff archaeologist at the Illinois State Museum, arrived with a small crew of workers to see what they could salvage before Murdock proceeded. A quiet, dedicated professional, Smith conducted the first modern excavation at Cahokia—a noteworthy event because in the 1940s it was unusual to have a woman dig director.

Through the summer and fall of 1941, Smith and her crew determined that Murdock Mound contained 13 layers. They realized they were uncovering a heavily used ceremonial area, including the remains of many well-constructed, grass-thatched buildings, possibly temples or houses of the elite. Inside the buildings were central fire pits and benches measuring about two feet across.

As the crew excavated the remains, they discovered one building that was different from the others. Rather than being rectangular, it was round, with walls twice as thick as the surrounding houses, and it contained a much deeper fire pit. The clay in the fire pit had burned intensely, indicated by its deep red color, suggesting that fires had been kept going over long periods of time. A large rectangular house stood seven feet from the round building. Smith suspected that the round building had been a sweatlodge (a small, heated, ceremonial structure) or a temple with an eternal flame. Possibly the adjacent building was the residence of a chief or priest.

Smith's careful observations showed that all the one-room houses, through all levels of occupation between 1050 to 1250 CE, were on a north-south axis. In addition, their sides were parallel to the sides of Monks Mound. She realized that even though the builders of Cahokia did not have writing, they must have built their houses, temples, and pyramidal mounds according to a thoughtfully constructed master plan.

Her work came to an end in December of 1941, when the United States entered World War II. The dig was put on hold until the war ended, but Smith never returned to the project to analyze

The neighborhoods at Cahokia were composed of groups of related families. In this re-creation of a summer day, children play games, women grind corn, and others are off hunting, fishing, farming, and thatching roofs.

Archaeologists Preston Holder (left) and Bell Cole excavate one of Cahokia's mounds in 1956.

the potsherds her crew found. Her finds still remain in storage, waiting for future Cahokia archaeologists.

There was some archaeological work at Cahokia through the 1950s, but none of it was very extensive. Part of the problem was Cahokia's size. Universities had neither the money nor the staff to excavate several square miles of pyramidal mounds that extended from Cahokia into East St. Louis, west across the Mississippi River, and into St. Louis. Pot hunters, unauthorized diggers, and—most damaging of all—developers of houses, shops, and factories continued to threaten the remains.

Only two or three archaeologists kept regular watch on the Cahokia area during this period. One of these was an unconventional archaeologist named Preston Holder, who taught at Washington University in St. Louis. A handsome, dynamic man, Holder may have been unconventional because he grew up in a circus.

Holder investigated Cahokia and its surroundings whenever he heard that a farmer turned up some archaeological evidence. In 1956, he obtained a grant to excavate the largest of a row of six mounds that mark the northern boundary of the Cahokia site. This mound was about to be leveled for the construction of a bridge.

Holder did not like what he called the "telephone-booth-excavation mentality"—the then-standard practice of digging five-by-five-foot pits to test the soil for evidence. He took a different approach. He excavated a large area so that he could see the floors of the temples and houses atop the long-buried levels of this flat-topped mound. As he uncovered part of the mound, he immediately saw evidence of many ancient temples, residences, storehouses, and sweatlodges.

Cahokians would construct temples and houses on top of the flat mound, and then, the following year, they would tear them down and rebuild them after carefully prepared earth was added to make the mound higher. They did this around harvest time in the late summer. The floors of the houses and temples were painted red, and elaborately woven cattail-reed mats covered the walls and the floors. Inside they lived, prayed, planned for the future—and made shell and bone-bead necklaces. The site also included implements of sandstone and flint, bone awls, pieces of woven fabric, and numerous shell fragments from the Gulf Coast.

This pottery cup, from an area a half mile west of Monks Mound called Tract 15A, is engraved with a cross-and-circle symbol.

Through the 1950s, construction of modern subdivisions, discount stores, and parking lots continued to threaten the ancient mounds. The Gilcrease Museum in Tulsa, Oklahoma, and the Illinois State Museum sent archaeologists to dig into small platform mounds where objects made of shell, copper, and crystals were found. These mounds, like Holder's, had begun small and had grown large over time as Cahokians worked to make them bigger. Smith, Holder, and the other archaeologists' findings showed that Cahokia was a complicated urban center.

Then, in the 1960s, a federal interstate highway program began in the Cahokia area. As the ground was cleared for the highway, archaeologists conducted salvage excavations of Cahokia to save any remains that would otherwise be destroyed at Cahokia and its outlying villages. They had to move quickly to stay ahead of the

Before a foot of the top soil was removed from an area named Tract 15B (left), the land looked ordinary. Once it was stripped (right), archaeologist Warren Wittry and his crew were amazed to see the dark stains of archaeological features everywhere in the bare earth.

bulldozers that seemed always ready to roll in. Unfortunately, the federal highway department set restrictions on the work that made excavating difficult. It insisted that the archaeologists maintain a strict timetable and that the crews keep within the proposed highway boundaries, no matter how important a find they came across.

Despite the highway department rules, archaeologist Warren Wittry and his team dug all of what they called Tract 15B, a 15-acre tract 300 yards west of Monks Mound. Tract 15B showed that houses had been built over several generations, until finally a large walled compound was constructed over the former neighborhood. As the team went on to excavate Tract 15A, another 15-acre tract 1,000 yards west of Monks Mound, Wittry found the remains of nearly 200 houses and hundreds of filled-in pits. He called some of these pits "bathtubs" because of their shape. He found that these bathtub pits had large stains in the soil, which indicated that the ends of large, upright posts had once stood at the spot. Mapping their finds, the team realized these former post foundations were arranged in huge circles. Wittry called them

Archaeologists have discovered that Cahokians built large circles made of wooden posts, which they call woodhenges. Evidence suggests Cahokians may have used these structures as part of rituals that celebrated the arrival of summer and winter.

"woodhenges" after the remains of wood circles that were uncovered in western England.

When archaeologist Timothy Pauketat reexamined the findings in 1989, he found that these huge post circles had been built over the top of earlier Cahokia houses, evidence of a kind of urban renewal. At least one of the circle constructions seems to have astronomical alignments; the rising sun aligns with various posts at different times of the year. Another archaeologist proposed that the woodhenges could have been the sites of important Cahokian rituals not unlike the sun dances or celebrations of the rebirth of the world performed by Indian tribes who lived on the Great Plains in later times. Yet woodhenge posts have not been found at other Mississippian sites. One of the largest buildings at Cahokia stood just north of one of the woodhenges. Second in size only to the enormous structure on top of Monks Mound, its placement emphasizes the importance of the woodhenges to the Cahokians.

Emergency Archaeology

Hurry! Construction workers grading away a hillside have just uncovered an ancient village! There are bones, potsherds, stone tools, a rare carved stone smoking pipe, and the dark stains that look to have been the locations of former houses from 1,000 years ago. By next week, the site will be gone. Grab your trowels and brushes, your surveying equipment, as well as your pencils and pens, blank graph paper and forms. This is the equipment you need to dig, sift the dirt, uncover the artifacts, and record information before the construction workers destroy the evidence.

It is sometimes difficult to believe that this kind of "salvage" archaeology still occurs today in the middle of the United States; one might think that the cultural heritage of the people of the past would be protected by law. However, so much urban development is happening now that important archaeological sites are always being eaten away, destroyed by the hungry forces of "modern progress." Large parts of the Cahokia site and countless outlying farming village sites have been destroyed in the recent past. Since the 1970s, federal and state laws have been written to protect many sites.

During "salvage" archaeology, the crew has to get as much information as they can before the deadline enforced by the state highway department runs out. Often bulldozers are ready to move in as archaeologists hastily finish their work.

The best archaeological excavations to occur in the Midwest were conducted by archaeologists working with or for state highway departments, state parks, and other federal construction projects. These "cultural resource management" efforts were carefully planned and have given us detailed knowledge of the past. Yet the need to rescue some sites quickly persists, and the incredible value of archaeological remains is still under appreciated by many. Federal and state laws protect many sites—but not always.

4

Evidence Accumulates

Archaeological evidence shows that Cahokia was a great ceremonial center where important chiefs, families, and clans lived. There are larger mounds and smaller mounds, possibly telling us that some Cahokian clans were bigger in size and had more labor power available, while others were smaller and less important. Some families were given special treatment at death, as seen in the evidence of elite rituals that have been found in Cahokia's unique ridge-top mounds. Ridge-top mounds were long mounds, originally flat-topped earthen pyramids, converted into different shapes to look like the "house of the dead" for the burials of Cahokia's upper-crust society.

Mound 72, located a half-mile south of Monks Mound, was one of only two ridge-top mounds within the boundaries of the park in 1967. Over the years, others had been destroyed for various reasons.

An artist re-created this scene of a Cahokian chief (center) and his priests atop Monks Mound as they greet the sunrise.

But observers spotted burial pits lined with skeletons every time people ruined a ridge-top mound. Mound 72 was small, only 140 feet long, 70 feet wide, and barely 6 feet high. It was oriented along a northwest-southeast axis. One end pointed to the winter solstice sunrise and the other toward the summer solstice sunset. In 1967, Melvin Fowler, supervising archaeologist of Cahokia excavations, decided Mound 72 should be investigated.

Fowler's career had begun as a surveyor and civil engineer. He suspected that Mound 72 and the other ridge-top mounds were markers of some kind. Could the big posts that had been discovered elsewhere on the Cahokia site, such as those on Tract 15A, be part of this marking system? Using his surveying skills by drawing gridlines and doing complicated geometry, Fowler was sure he could predict where other posts would be found.

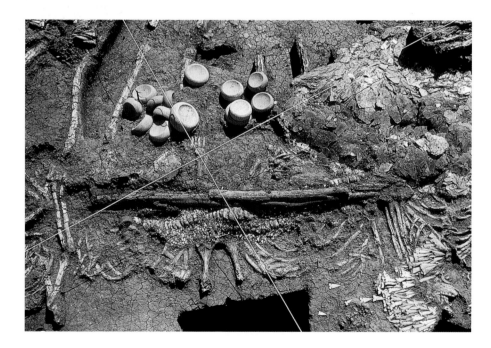

The complicated burial site called Mound 72 contained arrowhead caches (bottom right), as well as stone disks named "chunkey stones" (center) and piles of mica, hammered sheet copper, and strings of large shell beads (top right and center).

Incredibly that is just what happened. Fowler and his crew excavated where they predicted post pits would appear. Sure enough, there were the stains of the now-disintegrated upright posts in place. The wood dated to Cahokia's founding in 1050 CE. Fowler's posts were part of the thoughtfully constructed master plan that Harriet Smith had recognized 25 years earlier.

When the crew started excavating a new trench, they found a smaller, early stage of Mound 72. A black clay mixture, resistant to erosion, covered this mound. Kenneth Williams, a student who had been volunteering on archaeology projects since he was 14 years old, started cutting a trench into the black mound. He smashed his mattock (a tool with a two-foot handle and a sharp blade) about a foot into the mound. Black clay flew up. He looked down and there in the cut were three perfect arrowheads. Williams had almost shattered them. Quickly, the crew switched from mattocks to dental picks and dug very cautiously. Soon they uncovered hundreds of stone arrowheads.

When archaeologist Melvin Fowler first visited Cahokia in 1961, he stopped at a farm house to ask for directions. The owner had never heard of the mounds even though she was living around the corner from them.

The workers' excitement grew as they spotted layer upon layer of human bones beneath the stone tools. They had discovered a complex mortuary site that held the remains of hundreds of individuals. About three feet west of the pit were two groups of burials. In one, the main figure was the skeleton of a man lying face-up on a platform or blanket of about 20,000 drilled shell beads. During an archaeological conference, weeks later, Fowler showed a slide of this burial. Immediately, Patrick Munson, the former supervisor of

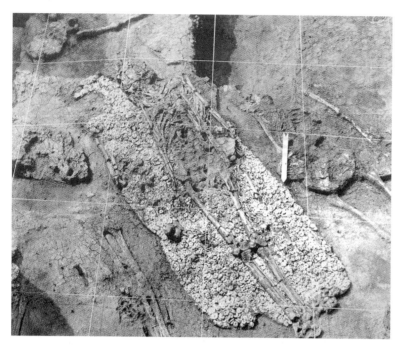

Melvin Fowler did not realize that the blanket made with about 20,000 shell beads, on which this skeleton lay, was in the shape of a bird.

Tract 15A dig, called out from the audience, "That's a bird. A beaded bird!" Despite Fowler's and his crew's careful scrutiny, they had not realized that the man had been placed on beads in a bird-shape, probably a falcon, or a "thunderbird." From then on the skeleton was known as the Beaded Birdman Burial.

Near the Beaded Birdman were the remains of three men and three women, all buried at the same time. Fowler suspected that if the Birdman was the chief of Cahokia, these skeletons could be his aides or companions who had been sacrificed with him. Beside these skeletons were exotic goods: wooden rods covered with copper imported from the Lake Superior region; shell beads; bushels of sheet mica from North Carolina; and more than 1,000 showpiece arrowheads chipped out of different stones from as far away as Arkansas, Tennessee, and Wisconsin. Several hundred of these had tipped, long-decayed arrows and appeared to be bundled together for burial with these high-status people. The most impressive of these burial goods were 15 beautifully polished stone disks, called "chunkey stones," measuring four to five inches in diameter. These stones, we know from later tribes, were important in sporting events that they called "chunkey," where teams gathered in plazas and wagered everything they owned on the roll of the stone.

The crew found still more skeletons under Mound 72: four men, arranged side-by-side with their arms overlapping. All four men were missing their heads and hands. Nearby, bones of more than 50 individuals lay side-by-side and were stacked in layers. A specialist concluded that they were all young women between the ages of 18 and 23. These women, in addition to women found in three more pits, had been executed during ceremonial events.

Surprisingly, the diet of these sacrificed women differed from others found at Cahokia. Calculations made from residue in their bones revealed that these women ate much more corn than normal. Experts suggest that these young women might have come from outlying farming villages and were used as human sacrifices.

Fowler's dedicated team excavated Mound 72 for four seasons, usually under the hot summer sun in temperatures of 100-plus degrees Fahrenheit. From the findings, Fowler concluded that Mound 72 was enormously complicated. Dating to shortly after 1050 CE, the contents of the burials give clues to how important Cahokian leaders demonstrated their power at the beginning of Cahokia's reign. The uncovered evidence shows a theatrical display of violent killings (beheading, severed hands), burials honoring the elite (the Birdman), mass sacrifices (the young women), and the burial of weapons, status symbols, and valuable gifts. These death rituals were probably only carried out for a short period of time, no more than 100 years. At the end of the era, this family of chiefs probably lost its influence. Perhaps the other destroyed ridge-top mounds were also shrines that paid tribute to different ruling families of Cahokians.

Archaeologists also investigated Monks Mound and found that that there had been a large building on top of this enormous,

Within Mound 72 was a huge cache of arrowheads (above), placed between the skulls of two burial plots. Made of local chert, flint-like rock, from quarries near St. Louis, they include typical Cahokian triangular forms and foreign Louisiana forms. Chunkey stones (below) were found near the arrowheads. They were rolled across plazas by players on opposing teams.

carefully layered pyramid. Below the summit, on its east side, another excavation crew hit what seemed to be a rock. But to their surprise, it was a four-inch by three-inch sandstone tablet sticking out of the dirt. There was cross-hatching on one side and an engraving of a falcon dancer on the other. The masked figure had a diamond eye, a hooked nose, and an oval ornament on his chest. The arms were feathered wings. This "birdman" has since become the logo of the Cahokia Mounds Interpretive Center and is reproduced everywhere around Cahokia.

At the same time as Fowler's crews were digging Mound 72 and Monks Mound, Charles J. Bareis, an enthusiastic and tireless archaeology professor from the University of Illinois, was excavating a bizarre deposit at Mound 51, which was on a privately-owned land outside the park boundaries. The owner had a sign posted announcing "Indian Mounds for Sale," and was selling its dirt to local residents for landfill.

In 1966, Bareis and his team worked on Mound 51 with a backhoe that scooped very deep. A student far down in the pit spied a bone harpoon-tip. The piece of harpoon turned out to be at the top of a 10-foot-deep former borrow pit filled with the foulest, smelliest debris ever found at Cahokia—they had discovered what had been a huge garbage dump.

Bareis dug large telephone-booth squares down to the bottom of the debris, where artifacts were well preserved because of the airless depth. One-thousand-year-old wooden tools had not disintegrated; pumpkin seeds looked like they had just been scooped from a jack-o-lantern; remains of beetles, ants, and maggots

Excavating Monks Mound, archaeologists uncovered a sandstone tablet with this masked figure. This "birdman" has become the symbol of Cahokia, even appearing on the area's highway overpasses.

were imprisoned in the foul garbage. Large pieces of broken pots had been swept into the pit. Also recovered were beautifully preserved animal bones, tobacco seeds, exotic arrowheads, crystals, and a shell-bead necklace similar to artifacts from Mound 72.

Years later, a team of researchers led by Timothy Pauketat sorted through storage boxes of finds from the garbage dump site. They rediscovered the remains of what had been enormous ceremonial feasts held between 1050 and 1100 CE. The pit was more than 150 feet long, 60 feet wide, and 10 feet deep, and it contained layers of remains from feasts, with parts of hundreds of deer, fish, and birds, thousands of broken cooking pots, and tens of thousands of seeds, berries, and bits of tobacco. The archaeologists realized that each feast was probably attended by hundreds, if not thousands, of the first Cahokians. They danced, worshiped, smoked, and ate. When they were finished, they swept aside the remains into the pit.

Farmers coming into Cahokia's center from outlying villages were probably carrying hundreds of deer, fish, and birds, and stewing untold gallons of seed porridge and pumpkin soup for the feasts. They smoked tobacco, worked on the mounds and temples, and then returned to their homes. But despite all this evidence, the questions remained who were these farmers? Did they have anything to do with the rise and fall of Cahokia?

The experts had to wait a while longer to get those answers. A second highway project was initiated and conducted from 1979 through 1982. But now new national laws enabled archaeologists to better protect the site and its artifacts. In 1979, archaeologist Bareis signed an agreement with the Illinois Department of Transportation and the Federal Highway Administration to supervise the excavation of 59 archaeological sites.

This phase of the digging showed that in earlier times, there were dozens of Woodland Indian villages and campsites across this stretch of the Mississippi River Bottoms. But why were there only scattered farmsteads by Cahokian times? Archaeologist Tom Emerson, who took over the dig after Bareis retired in the 1990s, believes Cahokians encouraged farmers to spread out and farm more land than they had before. Several small red stone statues, found from excavations on the outskirts of Cahokia, indicated highly skilled artisans had made carvings of people, supernatural beings, and important crops. These objects reflect how necessary crop production was to the Cahokians. And yet these objects made at Cahokia were given away to farmers during special ceremonies or feasts. Emerson and Pauketat concluded from this evidence that Cahokian leaders encouraged thousands of people to come together as part of a new religious cult that swept the Mississippi River Bottoms.

A small refuse pit in cross-section shows how archaeologists would dig its layers of dirt and artifacts. At first, the pits were used by Indians as underground refrigerators for food storage. Later, they would be converted into trash dumps.

In 1995, another site was discovered that has updated archaeologists' thinking about the role of Cahokia's outlying farmers. Archeologists Timothy Pauketat and Brad Koldehoff heard about a local man who was finding broken pottery on the edge of a subdivision that might date to the Mississippian period. The two archaeologists had grown up in the hilly farmland of southwestern Illinois, and as boys, they had enjoyed collecting Indian arrowheads. When they met with the local man, he had just found a broken stone smoking-pipe with a human head and a snake etched on its side. To their surprise they saw the remains of a dozen partially bulldozed Mississippian houses. Pauketat eventually uncovered 60 more houses at this one site.

Since then, Koldehoff and Pauketat have discovered at least ten such farming villages along with uncounted dozens of smaller farmsteads and hamlets in the hilly uplands away from the Mississippi River Bottoms. Nearly all of them appear to have been founded at the same time as the Cahokian city at 1050 CE and are presently threatened by urban sprawl.

A University of Illinois graduate student, Susan Alt, who has studied 250 house remains from five of the sites excavated by the university since 1995, found that these villages were part of Cahokia's master plan. These farmers helped build Cahokia and were the people who carried in the foods to the great feasts. Perhaps these were the villages of the sacrificed women found in Mound 72.

But Alt and Pauketat are beginning to wonder whether these hill farmers were content with the elaborate rituals of nearby Cahokia. These people's old-fashioned pottery and house styles suggest an unwillingness to change with the times. The farmers may have been unhappy with Cahokians. In fact, only 100 years after the founding of the villages and the building of Cahokia's new pyramids and plazas, the people left the villages and farmsteads.

Tom Emerson became chief archaeologist for the University of Illinois's highway archaeology program after the retirement of Charles Bareis in the early 1990s. He has been a leader in interpreting Cahokia's "dispersed villages."

The Power of Pots

Pottery had been used along the Mississippi River for at least 2,000 years before Cahokians appeared on the scene. At the height of Cahokia, expert potters lived at and around Cahokia, and these women potters (and perhaps men) made fancy, delicate dishware for special ceremonial occasions. Some of the finest pots made in North America were made at Cahokia.

Archaeologists named these jars, bowls, beakers, plates, and cups "Ramey Incised," "Monks Mound Red," and "Powell Plain." Cahokians usually decorated the pots by carefully carving, etching, or incising the drying clay before the pots were fired to harden them. Some of the decorated pots were used by Cahokians to dispense potions, medicines, or special ritual foods to farmers who had come to Cahokia for the great ceremonies that took place.

Cahokians used pots to cook, store, and serve food and drink. They made them in many different shapes and sizes.

The carved, etched, or incised symbols on certain of these pots have been interpreted by archaeologists to be an early form of pictographic writing. These pictograms told the user how she or he fit into the grand natural design of things and how supernatural powers were managed by Cahokians. Some of the symbols represented the eyes and tail feathers of thunderbirds—great supernatural sky gods. There were other designs that depicted the sun, the four cardinal directions, rainbows, and even the spirals of seashells.

5

The Great Ceremonial Center Disintegrates

As the ground for the new Cahokia Mounds Interpretive Center, designed to tell Cahokia's story to the public, was prepared in 1985 and 1986, archaeologists from Southern Illinois University discovered the foundations of dozens of houses. They found that all the houses, except for the ones built after 1150 CE, were aligned according to the master grid, as Harriet Smith had suspected. These later houses were angled and spaced in less predictable ways. By that time each family was making up its own mind about how and where to build. What had changed?

The first piece of that puzzle was found years earlier, in 1968. Archaeologist Melvin Fowler spotted an area on aerial photos that

Archaeologists conduct excavations before building the Cahokia Mounds Interpretive Center. They later found that the site had three previously unknown mounds and a residential neighborhood that determined how the Center would be shaped.

showed a strange light-colored line running alongside Monks Mound and up toward the future museum site. When the crews first dug in the area, they found parts of a huge wooden wall. Built and rebuilt between 1150 and 1200 CE, it was 15 feet high and encircled 300 acres. Archaeologist William Iseminger, a longtime Cahokia investigator, estimated that the trunks of 20,000 trees, each less than a foot in diameter, were used to build the enormous wall, sometimes called a palisade wall because the logs are placed close together to form a defensive enclosure. In addition, platforms for archers projected from the wall every 200 feet. Arrows could have been shot down from these platforms onto anyone who might attempt to scale the wall. By this time, it seems, Cahokians needed to defend themselves.

The massive wall was built right through the middle of Cahokia's open plazas, cutting off views, separating neighbors, and making a clear distinction between what happened inside the wall and what happened outside. Along with the houses built with little regard to Cahokia's master plan, the finding of the wall convinced archaeologists that the Cahokian social order and its master plan

Archaeologists shovel across the palisade trench, the dark stain in the ground, revealed during the excavation.

were beginning to disintegrate. Soon after, another archaeologist found a different example of this same phenomenon at the top of a small mesa, 12 miles north of Cahokia. His team found houses dating to 1175 CE inside a small, fortified village.

In a more recent dig at what was left of the old East St. Louis site, crews of archaeologists found more clues. Amidst the high-status houses and large post pits and inside a modest palisade wall were a series of temples and storage huts that had burned to the ground. Inside the incinerated storage huts were whole pots, burned baskets full of maize, and still-usable wooden and stone tools left behind during this East St. Louis fire. The fire dated to around 1160 CE.

This information shows that the end of Cahokia's rule over the farmers of the Mississippi River Bottoms and surrounding hills was rooted to some extent in the threat of violence. Palisade walls, platform for archers, weaponry, and burned houses are signs of trouble. More important, the farming villages excavated by Susan Alt and Tim Pauketat were abandoned at the same time that the palisade walls were being built. Cahokians began to leave the region beginning in 1150 CE. By 1350 CE, there were no Mississippian peoples left in the Mississippi River Bottoms. Cahokians had always relied on the foods and the labor force that came from their farmer neighbors. Once the farmers left, Cahokia fell apart.

A re-creation shows the center of Cahokia enclosed by the enormous palisade wall. Built between 1150 and 1200 CE, it had regularly spaced platforms and encircled some 300 acres.

By the time the first Europeans arrived in the 16th century, Cahokia was uninhabited. Archaeologists now think that Cahokia's people broke up into numerous groups over the next two centuries and emigrated to other parts of America. French, Spanish, and American explorers to the area encountered the Osage, the Ponca, the Omaha, and other groups of Indians west of the Mississippi River. These native peoples played chunkey, had elaborate ritual feasts, formed sacred organizations, and were led by hereditary chiefs—all echoes of Cahokian culture. The blood of at least some of Cahokia's descendants probably courses through the veins of some of these Indians.

When the Cahokia Mounds Interpretive Center opened in 1989, it became a living tribute to the archaeologists, both professional and amateur, who over the years insisted that this was more than just a group of unimportant Indian mounds. Rather, it was a significant historic site that should be preserved for the future. Cahokia lay at the heart of a grand chiefdom, a North American city-state whose farmers were just as important as its chiefs and nobles.

The Interpretive Center at Cahokia Mounds State Historic Site was built so that people can learn about Cahokia's history and the people who lived there.

Interview with Timothy Pauketat

Nancy Stone Bernard: You mentioned that when you were growing up in the hilly farmlands of southwestern Illinois, you collected arrowheads. Was that the experience that led you to a career in archaeology or was there something else?

Timothy Pauketat: Collecting arrowheads was definitely a big part of my choice of archaeology as a career. But most arrowhead collectors don't become professional archaeologists. For me, the real reason I went into archaeology was my parents. My mom, Janet, instilled in me a love of genealogy and natural history. In fact, she herself had collected rocks and arrowheads from her family's farm. My dad, Bobby, became a bigger arrowhead enthusiast than I and took me camping and fishing regularly. There were lots of other important experiences too, without which I wonder if I'd have stuck with archaeology as a career. I veered into geology in college, but an archaeology field school and then a job as a student intern with the Corps of Engineers gave me the needed confidence and know-how to move on to graduate school at Southern Illinois University and then at Michigan.

NSB: When you were an undergraduate at college, did you have an idea of what kind of archaeology you would like to do?

Archaeologist Timothy Pauketat (top) and writer Nancy Stone Bernard (bottom, at a Mississippian mound).

TP: You bet. I remained focused on trying to understand Cahokia from the first day that I saw the big pyramid, Monks Mound, when I was seven or eight years old. I used to accompany my dad to his work, which was driving a delivery truck. On Tuesdays he would drive past Cahokia Mounds, so even as a little boy I went along specifically to see Cahokia. By the time I made it to college, I was as much excited by paleontology and hard-rock geology as by archaeology. I never thought I'd become a professor because I was shy, and standing up in front of 100 people in a classroom made my heart jump. I had considered going into historic archaeology, geoarchaeology (the combination of geology and archaeology), and even into the study of early civilizations in Africa. But in the end Cahokia was still in my head, and one project led to another, seeing me all the way through my doctoral degree and leading to my job as a professor!

NSB: For many years you've taken your students to dig at Cahokia. Can you explain what you do and the difficulties of summer field schools at Cahokia?

TP: We are studying the origins of civilization in North America. I want to know the story of who built Cahokia and how they did it because the answers to those questions have a bearing on understanding all North American history—even the history of the United States itself. So,

we've dug into Cahokia's central plaza and one of its mounds to find evidence of when and how it was built, and we've dug at a few outlying towns to see whether or not these too were built at the same time by the same people. But most recently we've discovered a series of outlying farming villages that had been filled with people who were growing food for themselves and, probably, for the Cahokians.

Digging in any place at or around Cahokia has a set of unique challenges. First and foremost, it's often incredibly hot and humid, rivaling places in the tropics in its extremes. Sometimes students go down with heat exhaustion. Worse, there can be bad air and water pollution near Cahokia. Once we were digging at a site where the air pollution was so bad one day that our eyes and throats were burning—probably with sulfur dioxide.

But I guess the worst challenge to archaeology is the problem of site destruction. So many people, so many corporations, don't care about the past. They'd rather wipe it out, bulldoze it away, or build a housing subdivision on top of it than learn from it. Too many people in the United States don't value the past, especially the Native American past, because it seems irrelevant to their own present world. We need to prove them wrong.

NSB: What was your most memorable or exciting discovery?

TP: I've been involved in digging two ancient burned houses where all the possessions of the people had been left inside at the time of the burning. Whole smashed pots, chipped-stone knives and hoe blades, bone needles, half-cooked meals left on the floor as the residents left the house. These are like finding a miniature Pompeii, which is incredible when you realize you have a moment of one family's life from 1,000 years ago virtually frozen in time.

Perhaps my most memorable discovery was made with my students in 2001—a huge cache of stone axe heads—a rare find. Most of them were new when buried, and all were made from an imported rock that originates deep in the Ozark Mountains many miles southwest of Cahokia. By accident, a field-school student scraped across the first of them and was pretty excited. Of course, we all were. We crowded around the pit and each took turns uncovering what we at first thought was just a few axe heads. The 10-year-old daughter of the field director was helping us that day. She kept a running count, and by the end of the day, with the sun setting, we had pulled out 70 of them, including the biggest one ever found in place, at 25 pounds. As it turns out, these seem to have been a special ritual deposit buried in front of a big temple building at the edge of the village.

NSB: What is your advice to a young person who wants to make archaeology a career?

TP: Do it. It takes a love of the past along with a burning desire to actually *do* archaeology. Doing it isn't always easy, but if you love it enough, doing archaeology is the most fun you'll ever have. That's because you bring the lives of people long gone, with histories unwritten, back to life. Their stories are important! Nine-tenths of all human history is waiting to be discovered by us archaeologists. Going to school to become an archaeologist may seem long and drawn out, but in reality you are doing archaeology as you go. It involves reading, traveling, sweating, and laughing under difficult conditions. And you are constantly discovering new ideas along with artifacts from the past. So, I wonder if we shouldn't all be archaeologists, whether it's as a profession or as a hobby. Do it well and do it with all the hopes and dreams that you have. If that's the way you do it, possibly anything you want to know about the past you will be able to discover.

Glossary

Archaic Indians The name for various hunting and gathering Indians who established seasonal camps between 8000 and 1000 BCE across North America; they built the first mounds on the continent in present-day Louisiana.

Bering Land Bridge Part of the continental shelf that links the Russian Far East and Alaska.

borrow pits Cahokians dug in these places to get the dirt they used to build their mounds. Some of these holes became pools of water; others were filled to make extraordinarily leveled plazas.

chiefdom A large society with a form of government based on ruling chiefs. Often prestige is determined by how closely one is related to the chief.

chunkey A prehistoric Indian game played in the midwestern United States. A player rolled a stone disk as far as possible as the opponents threw spears at the point where they predicted the disk would stop.

city-state An independent city that has control over its surrounding territory.

effigy mound An earthwork created to represent a geometric form or a human, animal, or bird.

Mississippi River Bottoms East of present-day St. Louis, Missouri, the flat, fertile plain of the Mississippi River, which is intermixed with wet, swampy lowland, and frequently floods during the spring.

Paleo-Indians The name given to the first people to enter the New World from Asia. They spread slowly through North America and finally to South America.

plaza Public squares without houses. Cahokia's "Grand Plaza" is the largest such open square north of Mexico.

pre-Columbian A term referring to the time before Christopher Columbus landed in the New World. Sometimes called "prehistoric."

salvage archaeology Emergency archaeological excavations on sites that are scheduled to be destroyed by construction projects.

shaman A Native American religious leader. The term has also come to mean a prehistoric priest in the Old World as well.

solstice In the Northern Hemisphere, either the longest day of the year (June 21), also called midsummer, or, in winter, the shortest day of the year (December 21).

Thunderbird A Native American mythical supernatural being or deity that lived in their sky-world. Its eye and wing feathers were often shown on Cahokia's ceremonial pots.

woodhenge A circle of cedar posts that the Cahokians used for sky watching, or possibly to mark a sacred area. Cahokia is the only Mississippian site with this kind of structure.

Woodland Indians The name given to Native American cultures that developed after about 1000 BCE throughout most of eastern North America. The people lived in villages; grew crops including squash, corn, and pumpkins; made pottery, and established trading networks. In some places, they built dozens of earthen mounds and buried their dead with many artifacts within the mounds.

Further Reading

Chappell, Sally A. Kitt. *Cahokia: Mirror of the Cosmos*. Chicago: University of Chicago Press, 2002.

Debelius, Maggie, and the editors of Time-Life Books. *The First Americans*. Alexandria, Va.: Time-Life Books, 1992.

Fagan, Brian M. *The Great Journey: The Peopling of Ancient America*. New York: Thames and Hudson, 1987.

Iseminger, William R. "Mighty Cahokia." *Archaeology*, May/June 1996, pp. 30–37.

Johnston, Darcie Conner, and the editors of Time-Life Books. *Mound Builders and Cliff Dwellers*. Alexandria, Va.: Time-Life Books, 1992.

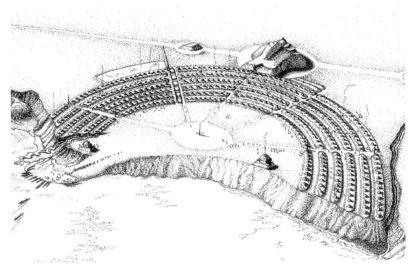

Mink, Claudia Gellman. *Cahokia: City of the Sun*. Collinsville, Ill.: Cahokia Mounds Museum Society, 1999.

Sattler, Helen Roney. *The Earliest Americans*. New York: Clarion, 1993.

Thomas, David Hurst. *Ancient North America*. New York: Thames and Hudson, 2000.

————. *Exploring Native North America*. New York: Oxford University Press, 2000.

Young, Biloine Whiting, and Melvin L. Fowler. *Cahokia: The Great Native American Metropolis*. Urbana: University of Illinois Press, 2000.

Cahokia Mounds and Related Sites in the American Midwest

CAHOKIA MOUNDS STATE HISTORIC SITE, ILLINOIS

(618) 346-5160

www.cahokiamounds.com

Cahokia Mounds State Historic Site was designated a UNESCO World Heritage site and a National Historic Landmark by U.S. Department of Interior. The site preserves the remains of the central section of the pre-historic Indian city. It includes 68 of the original 120 earthen mounds and the Monks Mound at the center.

ANGEL MOUND STATE HISTORIC SITE, INDIANA

(812) 853-3956

www.angelmounds.org

This fortified Mississippian town was once the center of a powerful chiefdom. About 2,000 people lived here from 1100 to about 1450 CE.

AZTALAN STATE PARK, WISCONSIN

(920) 648-8774

www.dnr.state.wi.us/org/land/ parks/specific/aztalan/

This 21-acre site was a pre-Columbian Native American Mississippian village. Some experts think that Cahokians colonized it, even though it was about 300 miles away.

EFFIGY MOUNDS NATIONAL MONUMENT, IOWA

(319) 873-3491

www.nps.gov/efmo/

Within this historic site are 191 mounds, 29 in the form of bear and bird effigies and the rest in geometric forms.

EMERALD MOUND, MISSISSIPPI

(601) 446-6502

www.cr.nps.gov/aad/feature/ emerald/htm

This second-largest native American ceremonial mound in North America was built and used by the ancestors of the Natchez Indians from about 1250 CE. They abandoned it before the French arrived in 1682. The Natchez shifted their ceremonial center to nearby Grand Village where the Great Sun, their hereditary chief, lived.

MOUNDVILLE ARCHAEOLOGICAL PARK, ALABAMA

(205) 371-2234

http://moundville.ua.edu

A large Mississippian settle-ment occupied it from about 1100–1450 CE. Second only to Cahokia in size, it was a 300-acre village, built on a roughly square plan and pro-tected on three sides by a wooden palisade. Within the enclosure was a central plaza and 26 earthen mounds.

TOLTEC MOUNDS ARCHAEOLOGICAL STATE PARK, ARKANSAS

(501) 961-9442

www.cast.uark.edu/~shelley/html/ parkin/toltecvisitpg/html

This site was occupied from about 700 to 1000 CE. The 19th-century owner of the site mistakenly thought the Toltec, a Mexican native group, built the mounds, but investigations have proved that native North Americans built here.

WINTERVILLE MOUNDS, MISSISSIPPI

(662) 334-4684

www.mdah.state.ms.us/hprop/ winterville.html

An Indian ceremonial center from about 1000–1450 CE, it was the center of a chiefdom with at least 23 mounds. Today, 12 of the site's largest mounds, are part of a park.

Index

Pictures and captions are indicated by page numbers in **bold**.

Agriculture. *See* Crops
Alt, Susan, 35, 39
Arrowheads, **28–29**, **31**, 33–34

Bareis, Charles J., 32–34
Beaded Birdman Burial, 30–**31**
Bernard, Nancy Stone, **41**–43
Birdman tablet, **32**
Borrow-pit lakes, **13**, 32
Brackenridge, Henry, 6, 15
Burial goods, 11, **28**, **30–31**
Burials, 10, 27–31

Cahokia complex, 6–7, 12–16, **21**–22, **26**.
Cahokia Mounds Association, 17–18
Cahokia Mounds Interpretive Center, **37**–38, **40**
Cahokia Mounds State Historic Site, **40**
Ceremonial areas, 20, 27
Chunkey stones, **28**, 30–**31**, 40
Clark, William, 14–15
Cole, Bell, **22**
Conical mounds, **10**
Corn, 7, 12, 31
Crops, 7, 10, 12, 31–34

Earthworks, 10–11.
East St. Louis site, 15, 38–39
Effigy mounds, 11
Emerson, Tom, 6, 34–**35**
Excavations, 6, 12, **14**, 20, 22–24, **26**, 29, 33

Farmers, farming villages, 6, 11, 31, 33–35, 39–40
Feasts, 33–35
Figurines, 6
Fire pits, 20–21
Flat-topped mounds, 22–23, 27
Food, 7, 10, 12, 31, 33–35
Fowler, Melvin, 6, 28–**29**, 31–**32**, 37–38

Garbage dumps, 32–33, **34**

Highways, department, 23–24, **26**
Holder, Preston, 6, **22**, 23
Human sacrifice, 30–31

Indians. *See* Native Americans
Iseminger, William, 38

Koldehoff, Brad, 34

Lewis, Meriwether, 14–15

Master plan, 21, 29, 35, 37–38
Mississippian culture, 12–13, 34
Mississippi Bottoms, 6–7, 12, 34–35
Monks Mound, **8**, **13**, **16**, 19, 24, **27**, 31–**32**, 38
Moorehead, Warren King, 6, **17–18**
Mound 51, 32
Mound 72, 6, 27–**28**, 31
Munson, Patrick, 29–30
Murdock, Harry, 19
Murdock Mound, 19–20

Native Americans, 8–11, 13, 17, 40

Palisade wall, 6–7, **38–39**
Patrick, John J. R., 15–16, 18
Pauketat, Timothy, 6, 25, 33–34, 39, **41**–43
Platform mounds, **10**, 23
Population, 7, 39–40
Post pits, 24–25, 28–29, 39
Pottery, 10–11, **23**, 35–**36**
Poverty Point, Louisiana, **9**–10
Pyramids, **8**, 12–**13**, 15, 21, 35

Religion, 10, 25, 34, 40
Ridges, semicircular, **9**–10

Ridge-top mounds, **10**, 27–28, 31
Rituals, **25**, 35, 40

Salvage archaeology, 6, 20, 23–24, **26**
Smith, Harriet, 6, **20**–23, 37
Snyder, John Francis, 17–18
Statues, red stone, 34
Storehouses, 23, 39
Sweatlodges, 20–21, 23

Temples, 20–23, 33
Thomas, Cyrus, 16–17
Tract 15A, **23**, 28
Tract 15B, **24**
Trench excavations, 22, 29

Watson Brake site, Louisiana, 10
Williams, Kenneth, 29
Wittry, Warren, **24**
Woodhenges, 6, **13**, 24–**25**
Woodland Indians and villages, 7, 10–13, 34

Timothy Pauketat is professor of anthropology at the University of Illinois at Urbana-Champaign. He is the author of several books, including *The Archaeology of Traditions: Agency and History Before and After Columbus* and *Ancient Cahokia and the Mississippians*.

Nancy Stone Bernard has written *Stonehenge* and *Valley of the Kings* in the Digging for the Past series. She founded and is the director of the Archaeological Associates of Greenwich, Connecticut, a nonprofit organization dedicated to educating the general public about archaeology. She served for six years on the governing board of the Archaeological Institute of America as its education chair. She has taught continuing education classes in archaeology and an enrichment program in prehistory to pre-collegiate students, first in Los Angeles, California, and for many years in Greenwich, Connecticut. She is currently on the editorial advisory board of *DIG* magazine.

Brian Fagan is professor of anthropology at the University of California, Santa Barbara. He is internationally known for his books on archaeology, among them *The Adventure of Archaeology*, *The Rape of the Nile*, and *The Oxford Companion to Archaeology*.

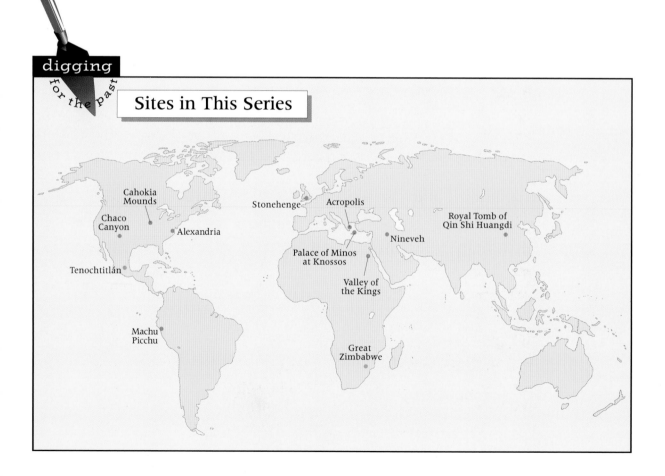

Sites in This Series

digging for the past

Cahokia Mounds
Chaco Canyon
Alexandria
Tenochtitlán
Machu Picchu
Stonehenge
Acropolis
Palace of Minos at Knossos
Valley of the Kings
Nineveh
Royal Tomb of Qin Shi Huangdi
Great Zimbabwe